POEMS
FOR
GREETINGS,
GIFTS AND
KEEPSAKES

POEMS FOR GREETINGS, GIFTS AND KEEPSAKES

For your
Hobby Craft, Card Making and
Scrapbooking Projects

Tracey Ann Prior

Photography by Callum Macdonald

First Edition
Gift Publishing

ISBN-13: 978-1479193059
ISBN-10: 1479193054

Cover Designed by Tracey Ann Prior
Photography by Callum Macdonald
www.callummacdonald.com

Dedicated To:

Gareth
Alex
Leanne
Andrew
Lauren
and
Megan

Whether you are creating a family history, a scrapbook page or a card for a friend, there is something delightful about making and giving a homemade gift. A simple poem and a little creativity can go a long way and really brighten someones day. I hope you enjoy the process and spread a little cheer along the way.

Contents

FAMILY, FRIENDS AND SPECIAL PEOPLE

Mother

You gave me life, you give me love,
You give so willingly.
You give me time, you lend a hand,
You do it cheerfully.
You have often been my compass
When I've not known where to go.
You have often been my anchor
When life's storms began to blow.
I value your opinion
And I often make it mine.
Life has taught you through its burdens,
While such skills I still refine.
Mum, I know you're human –
You are full of human ways –
Yet, the way you deal with problems
Fills my heart with awe and praise.
I have watched you in the sunshine,
Tears of laughter in your eyes.
I have seen, too, tears of sorrow –
Oh, how quiet were your cries.
Inside I carry with me
Precious memories from my past
When a warm and gentle mother
Gave me love enough to last.

Mom

You gave me life, you gave me love,
You gave so willingly.
You gave me time, you lent a hand,
And did it cheerfully.
Inside I carry with me
Precious memories from the past,
Where a warm and gentle mother
Gave me love enough to last.

Dad

You have been my inspiration
From the time my life began.
You're a wonderful example
Of a loving, caring man.
I've learned so much since childhood.
Your advice is sure and sound
And, as well as sharing wisdom,
You're such fun to have around.
I know I'm very lucky because, Dad,
You're very rare,
And I will always cherish
The great friendship that we share.

My Father

My father's broad shoulders
Have enabled him to bear
The burdens and the challenges
Of daily family care.
I know I'm very lucky
For my father's very rare,
And I will always cherish
The great friendship
that we share.

My Dearest Daughter

It seems like only yesterday
That you were in my arms.
A helpless little baby
Full of baby daughter charms.
From a little girl so caring
Came a woman warm and dear.
Someone capable and able
With a practised, listening ear.
You fill your life with labour –
Life demands a lot of you –
Yet you rise to every challenge
And give your best in all you do.
I'm so grateful for your friendship
And your lovely sense of fun.
I'm so proud, my dearest daughter,
Of the woman you've become.

Our Dearest Daughter

From a little girl so caring
Came a woman warm and dear.
Someone capable and able
With a practised, listening ear.
We're so grateful for your friendship
And your lovely sense of fun.
We're so proud, our dearest daughter,
Of the woman you've become.

Son, I'm Proud of You

The years have passed so quickly
That I wonder where they've gone,
But I know each year was worth it
When I see what you've become.
You are strong and independent,
In ways that good men are.
I no longer need to worry,
I can tell you will go far.
I love the man you are today –
The thoughtful things you do.
I don't say it very often
But, my son, I'm proud of you.

Son, We're Proud of You

The years have passed so quickly
That we wonder where they've gone,
But we know each year was worth it
When we see what you've become.
We love the man you are today –
The thoughtful things you do.
We don't say it very often
But, dear son, we're proud of you.

Lovely Husband

I'm so glad for the time
That I spend at your side,
For the husband you are to me;
For the fun and the love
That we share each day,
In a marriage that's meant to be.
I know that you honour
The promise you made:
You are faithful, committed and true.
I cannot imagine a happier life
Than spending each day with you.

My Lovely Wife

I remember the day that you
Stood at my side,
Whilst pledging your love to me.
A hopeful and radiant, beautiful bride –
It's a vision I always see.
I'm not always good at expressing my love,
But it deepens with each passing year.
I want you to know
That my love will go on.
I'm happy just knowing you're here.

Sister (or Brother)

We have laughed together, cried together,
Worried, joked and sighed together,
Learning life's great lessons
In a simple, natural way.
We have sparred as bitter rivals,
First with fists and then with words.
We have learned that love means doing,
And that fighting is absurd.
Siblings pull together,
Without thought and without doubt.
We just know that in a crisis
We must help each other out.
I don't say it very often
But you mean so much to me.
Dear sister, you are special
Because you're family!

My Grampy

A grand old father figure
Sleeping soundly in a chair,
A face of mellow quiet
With a peaceful, happy air.
I love spending time with you
And love to hear your tales,
Your take on worldly wisdom
And your smile that never fails.
I tell you all my problems
And you always give advice.
You just seem to have the answers,
Even though you give them twice.
I know how much you love me
And you know I love you too.
I'm so glad that you're my Grandad.
Grampy, thanks for being you!

Grandad, Here's a Handkerchief

Grandad, here's a handkerchief,
A little gift for you.
I know you use a handkerchief
In everything you do.
You wipe away our sorrow
And our tears of laughter, too.
Grandad, with this little gift
Comes lots of love to you.

Grandad

I know how much you love me
and you know I love you too.
I'm so glad that you're my Grandad.
Thanks for everything you do.

My Nana

Nana, when I think of you,
This is what I see;
The dearest, nicest Nana
Who thinks the world of me.
You share your wit and wisdom
In a warm and friendly way.
As you listen to my problems
And the mundane of my day.
Thank you, lovely Nana,
for the lovely things you do;
For being an example
And for simply being you.

Grandma

Grandma, when I think of you,
This is what I see;
A happy, smiling Grandma
Doing lovely things for me.
Your eyes are soft and knowing
As you sideways glance my way.
While you calmly sit there sewing
And I calmly sit and play.

I tilt my head like you do,
Your bifocals on my nose.
I'm not supposed to use them
But you don't mind while you doze.
Your words are laced with wisdom
And your humour's quick and dry.
You said you were a hundred,
I know now that's a lie!

Some people see your wrinkles –
I see your pretty face.
Some slow down to walk beside you –
I see a friend to race.
I'll always love you Grandma
Because you are are the best.
So mischievous a Grandma,
Better than the rest

Your Baby Girl (or Boy)

Nothing can replace the joy
A brand new life can bring.
Nothing will refine you more
Than love and nurturing.
Nothing can explain the hope
That little girls can bring.
And nothing can replace a child
Who means just everything.

Baby Girl

How blessed you are to have her.
She's on loan from Heaven above.
She brings so many blessings.
She will give you so much love.
You must teach her while she's little,
Nurture all the good you see,
And help this lovely baby
Be the girl she's meant to be.

Your Baby

Nothing can replace the joy
A brand new life can bring.
Nothing will refine you more
Than love and nurturing.
You'll find yourself developing
In ways you hadn't planned,
As you gaze upon your tiny child
And hold that tiny hand.
How blessed you are to have one
On loan from Heaven above
To bring you many blessings,
And give you so much love.
A destiny awaits, so
You must teach and you must guide.
And in return you'll gain a peace
That fills you deep inside.
No, nothing can replace the joy
That little ones can bring.
For nothing can replace the child,
Who means just everything.

Little Grandchild

There's nothing like a grandchild
To turn life upside down.
You're a precious little person
And a joy to have around.
Your lovely childish ways
Bring back so many memories
Of playing school, of skipping,
Building camps and climbing trees.
Of leaping like a kitten,
Not an ache, a thought, a care.
So innocent and happy,
Full of spirit, full of dare.
I crow about your talents
And your personality.
Grandchild, you are lovely
And you mean the world to me.

Our Family

Mother, Father, Daughter, Son.
Sacred words indeed.
Families bound by family love
Enabled to succeed.
Roots deeper than an ocean
Stretching from the dawn of time.
A golden chain unbroken.
That's our precious family line.
A home that's often Heaven
Heals the pain that life can bring.
It's worth our greatest effort –
Worth more than anything.

A Treasure Most Precious

A treasure most precious is each little child
In trust from our Father above.
An innocent, trusting, exuberant heart,
A source of great joy and great love.
A treasure most precious to each little child
Are mothers and fathers indeed,
Who cradle them up into safe, warm arms
And tend to their childhood need.
A treasure most precious are families –
The only safe haven we know.
Without them the world
Would be brought to its knees
And we would have nowhere to go.
Nothing compares to the bond of love,
A heavenly, magical glue.
Fathers are heroes and mothers divine
For a treasure most precious called you.

My Teacher

I may not be the quietest child
That you have ever known.
I know I tend to talk
Unless you sit me on my own.
I may not pay attention
Every minute of the day.
Admittedly, my favourite time
Is when it's time to play.
Relentlessly you teach me,
Not allowing me to rest,
Encouraging my efforts
As you make me do my best.
Some lessons are a challenge
And you teach me how to cope.
Each day I grow in confidence,
Ability and hope.
I sometimes see the progress
That I make from day to day,
But I can't see the foundations
That you're helping me to lay.
I guess I don't appreciate
The good that you have done.
I'm just glad you're my teacher,
For you make our lessons fun.

Teacher, You Are Leaving

I really have enjoyed the way
You've taught our class this year,
Your enthusiastic manner
And your sympathetic ear.
With skill you have encouraged me
To stretch and reach and try.
Your energy and confidence
Has inspired me to fly.
I remember witty comments
And a kind word here and there,
From a bright and helpful teacher
Who is fun and just and fair.
Now, though you must leave us
And move on to pastures new.
I would like to wish you happiness
In everything you do.

Teacher

Relentlessly you teach me,
Not allowing me to rest,
Encouraging my efforts
As you make me do my best.
I may not be the quietest child
That you have ever known.
I know I tend to talk
Unless you sit me on my own.
I guess I don't appreciate
The good that you have done.
I'm just glad you're my teacher
For you make our lessons fun.

I'm Glad You're My Friend

You take me as you find me
And accept my funny ways,
Are always full of sound advice
And generous with praise
I can talk to you quite freely
And you always understand.
You're prepared to roll your sleeves up
When I need a helping hand.
I'm at ease when I'm with you.
You're not easy to offend.
It's good to share such friendship
And I'm glad that you're my friend.

The Value of Friends

Who can determine
The value of friends,
As we travel life's path
As it winds and bends.
Our friends journey with us
Through happy and sad.
We laugh through the good times
And help through the bad.
People are fickle
And true friends are rare,
So we nurture the friendships
We're lucky to share.
I consider your friendship
As one of the best
And count myself lucky
In being so blessed.

MOTIVATION, ENCOURAGEMENT AND THANKS

Your Influence

Your influence has been
Most profound.
You helped me to walk
On solid ground.
You gave me direction
And set me straight.
You showed me the path
And opened the gate.
You dried my tears
And made me smile
And walked beside me
Mile after mile.
I love to listen,
You are just so wise,
And your friendship
Is something
I'll always prize!

Courage Within

It's hard to believe that the sun will shine
When the sky is a dark mass of grey.
But, honestly, you will see sunshine again,
And your troubles will seem far away.
You will get through it –
You can and you must.
You are much too strong to give in.
If you draw on your wisdom,
Your faith and your love,
You'll discover the courage within.

You're A Survivor

You're a survivor in life's great pond,
An achiever of wonderful things.
You weather your storms and
You always bounce back
As if lifted by angel wings.
I really admire your generous heart.
I see traces of something divine.
You're a light in the darkness, a beacon of hope,
And you're teaching me how to light mine.

A Big Thank You

I must say a very big thank you
For all that you've done and still do!
I don't know how I could have managed
Without someone as caring as you.
You've helped me to pick up the pieces
When I felt that I just couldn't cope.
You helped me to look to the future
With a sense of well being and hope.
I must say, again, a big thank you.
You've helped me in every way.
I'm so glad that your wonderful friendship
Enriches my life every day.

Thanks

Thanks for all you do for me,
For kindnesses each day.
It really means a lot, you see,
Although I may not say.
Life is so much nicer
Because of friends like you.
Thanks for being thoughtful.
Thanks for everything you do.

God Will Lift You

God is much closer than you are aware.
He listens and loves you.
He's sure and he's there!
He'll lift you and free you
From sadness and pain.
He'll show you that joy
Can be yours again.
If you give Him your heart
He will turn it around.
He will fill you with gifts
So that peace will abound.
He will change you
And build you and
Weave through your strife
A new pattern, new purpose,
New strength and new life.

He Will Lift You

When crisis tears down your security
And changes your life unalterably;
Then forces you forward into the unknown
As you desperately search
For your comfort zone;
Know God is much closer
Than you are aware.
He listens and loves you.
He's sure and he's there!
He'll lift you and free you
From sadness and pain.
He'll show you that joy
Can be yours again.
If you give Him your heart
He will turn it around.
He will fill you with gifts
So that peace will abound.
He will change you and build you and
Weave through your strife
A new pattern, new purpose,
New strength and new life.

Valuable You

Do you know from whence you came
And how special and golden you are?
You carry a vibrant and God-given flame,
A light that will carry you far.
When others disparage, believe they are wrong
For the message they send is untrue.
Discover your talents, your goodness, your love.
Let the world see the valuable you.

Action

We mustn't be spectators,
Always waiting in the wings.
We may not feel we're able,
But we can do many things.
Life is for the living
And it passes very fast.
Today's a day for action,
To participate at last.

A Day For Action

We mustn't be spectators,
Always waiting in the wings.
We may not feel we're able,
But we can do many things.
Some haven't been encouraged
And lack confidence to try,
While others are too frightened:
They won't reach or stretch too high.
Vanity and self-esteem
Are really not the same.
It's good to seek improvement,
To have purpose, to have aim.
Life is for the living
And it passes very fast.
Today's a day for action,
To participate at last.

Well Done

You did what you set out to do.
You aimed and worked
And saw it through.
Success is here – At last, it's true.
Well done! You did it!
Good for you.

Sunshine and Showers

Sometimes we can't see
The wood for the trees
And, try as we might,
We just can't seem to please.
We'd like to dissolve
All our problems away,
Imagining life filled with
Sunshine each day.
But life is a mixture
Of sunshine and showers.
If it weren't for the two
We would not have the flowers.
So instead of retreating
We must forge ahead,
Taking time to be happy
With each step we tread.

Endure and Fight

Oh, Blessed Father, hold me tight
And help me through this vale of night.
Within my heart a hope burns bright.
I must, I must, endure and fight.

Endure and Fight

If I can rise above the pain,
I have so many things to gain.
Today I am a wealthy child,
A richly blessed daughter mild.
My heart looks upwards to the sky,
And tries and tries so hard to fly.
My waking grief is hanging on
And heavily it pulls me down.
My wings beat harder and – surprise –
Despite the weight I start to rise.
Fragile wings support and guide
And sometimes when I need to glide
Another comes and lifts me high
And helps me soar and swoop and fly.
Oh blessed father, hold me tight
And help me through this vale of night.
Within my heart a hope burns bright.
I must, I must, endure and fight.

LOVE
AND
RELATIONSHIPS

Love Is The Sunshine

Love is the sunshine that lights up my life,
A sunshine which warms me through.
You are the sunshine that warms my heart.
You're so thoughtful and funny and true.
I know you are there at the end of each day
With a smile that's reserved for me.
There isn't a smile that I could love more,
Or a place where I'd rather be!

I Love You Totally

I guess I never realised
The joy that love could bring.
It's so powerful and potent
And it changes everything.
I sometimes can't believe it's me
By the things I do and say.
Incredibly, I didn't know
That love could be this way.
I can't begin to tell you
Just how much you mean to me.
You're my breath,
My thoughts,
My everything!
I love you totally!

My Greatest Treasure Is You

Life is so fabulously easy with you.
We walk together as best friends do.
You can be you and I can be me.
We are so close and yet we're so free.
We have our shared time
And our time alone.
We support one another
And each one has grown.
I have never sought riches
But now, it's true,
I'm rich! and my greatest treasure
Is you.

I'm Here

I don't want to step on private ground
But I care very much when you're down.
I'm not asking you to confide in me,
Simply letting you know I'm around.
I'd hate you to struggle on all by yourself
If you really could do with a friend.
There's nothing like sharing a problem or two
To unburden and lift and mend.

You Seem Distant

Is it my imagination
Or are you holding back from me?
You seem a little distant.
Is there something I don't see?
You know I really care for you.
So I hope there's nothing wrong.
If there is you must be honest.
Please don't keep me hanging on.

We Need To Talk

We need to be honest and open,
There are things that we need to say.
There are issues that need resolving
In a constructive and friendly way.
It's time we faced up to the problems
And tackled them one by one.
We will feel so much better tomorrow
When the talking and sorting is done!

A Bickering Ban

We have so much growing up to do,
Yet I know you care and I do too.
But put us together and before too long
We're quarrelling loudly
Which just seems wrong.
There must be something that we can do –
Some rules to help us calmly through.
I don't want a life this fraught and tense,
So to try and change it makes perfect sense.
If we work together and agree on a plan
I'm sure we can work out a bickering ban.

A Bickering Ban

We have so much growing up to do,
Yet I know you care and I know I do.
If we work together and agree on a plan
I'm sure we can work out a bickering ban.

Temptation

Everyone likes a lovely face,
A comely form that moves with grace,
An engaging smile and evocative charm,
A mild attraction that does no harm.
But flirtation can quickly get out of hand.
A fire will grow if it's fed and fanned.
Tears and regret are the price you could pay,
But with courage and love
You could just walk away.
Temptations will try to get through your defence,
But the grass isn't greener there over the fence.
You're standing on verdant
Green grass of your own
And soon you'll reap joy
From the love that you've sown.

Sorry I Hurt You!

At last I can see things clearly
And the sorrow I feel is immense!
It has taken this great upheaval
To finally make me see sense.
I'm so very sorry I hurt you.
This feeling is breaking my heart.
My life is so lonely without you.
I'm sorry that we are apart.

I'm Sorry

At last I can see things clearly
And the sorrow I feel is immense!
It has taken this great upheaval
To finally make me see sense.
I'm really sorry I hurt you.
I wish to reverse and undo.
I just hope that you can forgive me,
But I know it's not easy to do.

Sorry I Hurt You

At last I can see things clearly
And the sorrow I feel is immense!
I'm cross at my stupid behaviour
And my lack of old-fashioned good sense.
I'm so very sorry I hurt you,
And I'm filled with real tears of regret.
All I can do is to ask you
To try to forgive and forget.

I'm Miserable Without You

I miss you in the morning,
The beginning of my day.
The empty space beside me
Is apparent right away.
I miss you in the evening
When I settle down alone.
At times I feel so lonely
As I sit beside the phone.
They say that time's a healer,
But so far it isn't true.
I'm just miserable without you
And there's nothing I can do!

Miserable Without You

I miss you in the morning,
The beginning of my day.
The emptiness inside me
Is apparent right away.
They say that time's a healer,
But so far it isn't true.
I'm just miserable without you
And there's nothing I can do!

I Miss You

Your warmth, your voice, your smile, your kiss –
These are the things that I sorely miss.
I miss how your smile swept my worries away.
Your absence grows harder with each passing day.
I cannot relinquish our hopes and our dreams.
I cling to your memory through daily routines.
But my life is for living, although we're apart,
And we'll be together.
I know with my heart.

Missing You

Your warmth, your voice,
Your smile, your kiss –
These are the things
That I dearly miss.
I miss how your smile
Swept my worries away.
Your absence grows harder
With each passing day.
I cannot relinquish
Our hopes and our dreams.
I cling to your memory
Through daily routines.
But my life is for living,
Although we're apart.
I'm sad, and I miss you
With all of my heart.

Let's Pull Together

We made a commitment to walk side by side
Regardless of what lay ahead.
Sometimes it's tough and not quite as we planned,
And many real tears have been shed.
I want you to know that despite all the tears
I love you much more than you know.
I want to be with you and make our dreams real.
I know that we've further to go.
When we pull together and draw on our strengths
There is nothing that we can't achieve.
We have so much to gain, so much love to enjoy
If we dare to have faith and believe.

Time To Move On

The dust has settled. The business is done.
Our marriage is over, our new lives begun.
I know I am healing, I feel it each day,
But a deep-rooted feeling will not go away.
Time is a healer, but time's not enough.
I must be determined, and sometimes it's tough.
A sound or a smell can transport me away
To a wonderful moment, now so far away,
When life was so sunny and love was so new.
When you really loved me and I so loved you.
I have learned painful lessons –
I'm sure you have too.
And I wish us both joy in whatever we do.
There's a place in my heart
Where you'll always belong.
I miss you,
But it's time that my heart
Moved on.

Move On

The dust has settled.
The business is done.
The relationship's over.
New lives have begun.
My heart must be given
This chance to rebuild.
Love from the past
Must be reined in
And stilled.
A prisoner no more,
I am free to achieve
All that my hopeful heart
Dares to believe.

Our Marriage Is Over

The dust has settled. The business is done.
Our marriage is over, our new lives begun,
I know I am healing, I feel it each day,
But a deep-rooted feeling will not go away.
Time is a healer but time's not enough.
I must be determined, and sometimes it's tough.
A sound or a smell can transport me away
To a wonderful moment, now so far away,
When life was so sunny and love was so new.
When you really loved me and I so loved you.
In private reflection my subconscious screams
That I still hold your heart,
I still haunt your dreams.
My ego is trying to undo the done.
I know you don't love me and know you are gone.
I have learned painful lessons –
I'm sure you have too –
And I wish us both joy in whatever we do.
There's a place in my heart
Where you'll always belong.
But I know it's time for my heart to move on.

EVENTS AND OCCASIONS

Your New Home

May your new home be a happy place,
A sanctuary of peace,
A place where friendships blossom,
And unfriendly feelings cease,
A home of love and comfort,
A place where all find rest,
A place where friends are welcome:
A lovely home most blessed.

You're Eighteen

At eighteen, you're an adult
With a life to plan and build.
Good planning is the key
To seeing all your dreams fulfilled.
With a measure of intelligence,
A little common sense,
You must choose your own direction
For you own its consequence.
In time you will look back on
Your achievement and success,
So have a very special birthday
Filled with joy and happiness.

Graduation

Learning through study's a noble pursuit.
Your hard work and effort, at last, have borne fruit.
After reading, digesting and doing your best,
You now have the proof that you passed the test.
At your graduation you must be relieved,
For the goals that you set
Have now been achieved.
You have proved your potential
To learn and succeed.
Enjoy your success:
You have earned it indeed.

Graduation

At your graduation you must be relieved.
For the goals that you set have now been achieved.
You have proved your potential
To learn and succeed.
Enjoy your success: you have earned it indeed.

As You Retire

You have reached another milestone,
Long awaited, here at last.
It's time to change your lifestyle,
Not so hectic, not so fast.
This season is a special time –
It's time to think of you.
To concentrate your efforts
On the things you like to do.
To put old cares behind you,
A new season has begun.
You have years of work behind you
Now, at last, those years are done.
There is much that still awaits you,
Many skills you can acquire,
And a host of fondest wishes
Go with you as you retire.

Your Anniversary

When love was expanding and filling your life,
You made a choice to become man and wife.
Your promise was solemn and meant to be kept.
The fulfilment, yet future, you chose to accept.
In a world where a promise is lightly regarded,
You've nourished and cherished,
Protected and guarded.
With each year that passes, the promise bears fruit:
Your deepening love grows a much deeper root.
Each anniversary is time to reflect –
To look at each other with deeper respect.
You're growing a treasure that not many find:
A lifetime of marriage
As two hearts entwined.

Your 40th Anniversary

You have been through many seasons
And have shared a lot of years,
Have laughed together often
And have dried each others tears.
You've kept the solemn promises
Made forty years ago,
And your bond of love has blossomed,
And will shine and warm and grow.
Happiness together
Is the fruit that you now share.
You found the greatest treasure
In a marriage blessed and rare.

Your 25th Anniversary

You have been through many seasons
And have shared so many years.
You have laughed together often
And have dried each other's tears.
You have kept the solemn promise
Made just twenty years ago,
And the vows that you have honoured
Have acquired a silver glow.
Joy, love and devotion
Are the fruits of being loyal:
A lifelong transformation
Of a marriage blessed and royal.

Your Wedding

Masses of flowers and miles of lace,
Confetti and rice for your first embrace,
A band of gold and some photographs,
Best wishes and kisses and raucous laughs:
These are the things that you'll always recall.
The wonderful people, the fun of it all.
Enjoy every moment as man and wife.
Have a beautiful wedding
And a wonderful life.

Your Wedding

Masses of flowers and miles of lace,
Confetti and rice for your first embrace,
A band of gold and some photographs,
Best wishes and kisses and raucous laughs,
Sparkling glasses and wedding cake,
Smiling so long that your faces ache,
A mother awash with her handkerchief,
The speeches all done, such a sweet relief!
These are the things that you'll always recall.
The wonderful people, the fun of it all.
Enjoy every moment as man and wife.
Have a beautiful wedding
And wonderful life.

Our Wedding Promise

Our wedding is a covenant
We make from heart to heart.
A blessed and joyful union
Filled with blessings from the start.
We promise to be faithful
Until our lives are through.
We promise to be loving,
To be patient, chaste and true.
To make a home where both of us
Feel love and joy and peace.
A place where hope and confidence
Can steadily increase.
Our wedding is a special day,
Filled with love and prayer,
As we make our vows and covenants
For the life that we now share.

Your Wedding Promise

Your wedding is a covenant
You make with both your hearts,
A blessed and joyful union
Filled with blessings from the start.
You promise to be faithful
Until your lives are through.
You promise to be loving,
To be patient, chaste and true.
To create a home where both of you
Feel love and joy and peace.
A place where hope and confidence
Can steadily increase.
Your wedding is the joyful start
Of joyful days ahead.
It's a day you'll always treasure:
The day that you are wed.

I'm Getting Married Today

At dawn I awoke and gazed around
Absorbing the light, the sight, the sound.
I stared at the wedding dress on the door
And realised I would wake here no more.
I thought of the love and the fun I've had here,
Magical memories year after year.
"Thank you so much" seems too little to say.
I owe you so much. It's a debt I can't pay.
It's a life-changing thing
To become someone's wife,
But you're here in my heart
And still part of my life.

Our Best Man

We're grateful you were organised.
You checked and checked again,
Remembered what to say and do,
Each why and who and when.
We knew we could rely on you
By the caring you displayed.
We'd like to thank you heartily
For the vital part you played.

Thank You Bridesmaid

We truly want to thank you.
You'd a special part to play
In creating happy memories
On our precious wedding day.

Thank You Bridesmaid

The mention of a bridesmaid
Brings to mind a lovely rose,
All silk and lace and linen
Dressed with ribbons, pearls and bows.
Natural and elegant,
With flowers in her hair,
Adorned in simple splendour,
With a charm both warm and rare.
Each time we talk of bridesmaids
From now on, we'll talk of you.
You carried out your duty
With a smile the whole day through.
You were helpful and attentive
With an air of angel calm,
Spreading smiles and laughter
Like a wave of soothing balm.
We truly want to thank you.
You've a special part to play
In creating precious memories
On this, our wedding day.

My Baptism

Standing on the top step
And dressed in purest white
I advance into the water
With a feeling that it's right.
Buried are the old days,
The sorrows, the mistakes.
Emerging the new happiness,
Of which my soul partakes.
I feel my dearest Saviour
Beckoning to me
And rising through the water
I follow joyfully.
My burdens have now lifted
And my eyes can clearly see.
I am facing Heaven
With my life renewed and free.

Mary's Baby

Bethlehem was teeming,
There were people everywhere.
The couple searched for shelter,
But there was no shelter spare.
The husband knocked in earnest
As the woman clutched his arm.
She stopped. Her grip had tightened.
Joseph swallowed in alarm.
"We need a room, perhaps a stable,
For my wife is near her time."
With relief he led the donkey,
knowing now they would be fine.
Joseph quickly cleared the stable,
Laid a bedroll on the straw,
And in one heart-stopping moment
she gave birth upon the floor.
Mary held her brand new baby,
Like all mothers, filled with love.
She could feel the world rejoicing
And the joy from Heav'n above.
The Son of God, the Saviour,
The Redeemer of mankind
Was a helpless little baby
With a mother sweet and kind.
She laid Jesus in a manger
On a bed of stable straw,
Not knowing how her child
Would change the world for ever more.

Mary's Baby

Mary held her brand new baby
Like all mothers, filled with love.
She could feel the world rejoicing
And the joy from Heav'n above.
The Son of God, the Saviour,
The Redeemer of mankind
Was a helpless little baby
With a mother sweet and kind.
She laid Jesus in a manger
On a bed of stable straw,
Not knowing how her child
Would change the world for ever more.

Gethsemane

He knew this was the hour.
This was Gethsemane.
He was to be the saviour of all humanity.
Although he knew that mercy
Had a place in heaven's plan,
First, justice must be recompensed
And satisfied by man.
So, as his mortal friends lay sleeping,
He bowed low in solemn prayer.
While his sinless frame was tortured,
Racked with torment and despair.
He earned the right to offer mercy.
He became salvation's gate.
Whosoever lived his gospel
Could escape a sinner's fate.
He humbly left the garden
And took up his heavy cross.
His disciples watched in anguish,
Filled with sorrow at their loss.
But in days their sorrow left them
As their Master lived again.
And the resurrected Jesus
Offers heaven to all men.

Happy Easter

Easter is upon us,
Bringing proof that spring is here,
As sunny yellow daffodils
Fill every heart with cheer.
We spend our time with loved ones
And our gifts remain the same:
We give cards and chocolate figures
And play 'hunt the egg' again.
Our gifts are small reminders
Of the greatest gift of all,
When the Saviour gave his life for us
And saved us from the Fall.

THOUGHTS

My House May Not Always Be Tidy

My house may not always be tidy,
Although underneath it is clean.
The fridge isn't full of surprises,
But foods for a simpler cuisine.
The sticky young prints on the cupboards,
The free crayon art on the door,
Are touching and joyful reminders
Of the sweet little ones I adore.
No, this house is not always tidy,
But love makes this home heaven blessed.
A place of divine interaction,
A haven of safety and rest.

Blissful Reunion

Beholding in wonder a glittering city,
Having passed through lifes veil
Only moments before.
In awe at the gold and white clouds
In the heavens
While walking through flowers
On a glorious shore.
Drawn to the beautiful, heavenly singing.
Soothed by the gentle caress of the breeze.
Surrounded by life. All nature resplendent.
The healing, sweet scent
Of the blossom-filled trees.
Waves of pure joy now refreshing, renewing.
Oh, the rejoicing! Your soul is so thrilled.
Pure intelligence filling and lifting.
Soaring, absorbing. So whole. So fulfilled.
Finally, everything snaps into focus.
The groping in darkness has come to an end.
Your life had a pattern, a heavenly purpose.
You were shaped by a craftsman
And saved by a friend.
Two heavenly beings
Are walking towards you.
You instantly recognize maker and friend.
Warm arms enfold you in blissful reunion.
Your searching and yearning
Has come to an end.

Our Heritage

I'm warmed by quaint accents
And local traditions
And ruins that whisper of earlier days,
Moved by the challenge
Of modern conditions:
Which paths to abandon?
Which new trails to blaze?
Our land, touched by armies
Of talented craftsmen,
Hardworking, diligent
Women and men,
Great artists and writers
And brilliant draughtsmen,
And even a genius now and again.
A heritage forged
By the sweat of so many
Deserves to be cautiously added upon,
With tomorrow considered
And yesterday honoured,
Our legacy polished
And proudly passed on.

My Dear Departed Family

The years roll on relentlessly
And clouds obscure my memory
But beloved faces come to me:
My dear departed family.
Their struggles are now history
Compiled upon my family tree.
Their skeletons for all to see,
Laced richly with humanity.
Their tears and wars and harmony,
Their ignorance and illiteracy,
Intelligence and decency,
Their wisdom, wit and courtesy.
A large assembly watches me
And whispers from eternity.
Somehow I feel they're close to me
Anticipating eagerly.
I cannot stem my welling pride
For those who cried and tried and died.
Who persevered unsatisfied
And now in bliss reside.

An Empty Page

Each day is like an empty page.
Upon it goes our lives.
A thick and heavy catalogue
Listing lows and highs.
The twists of plot are varied.
Each consequence is seen.
Thoughts and acts in detail.
Who I am and where I've been.
Each page begins anew each day
And as I form each letter
I try to learn from yesterday
And live a little better.

A Pillow Made of Feathers

I lay my muddled head
Upon a pillow made of feathers
I rapture in its softness
As I close my tired eyes
A wave of jumbled thoughts spills out
Unhindered on the bed
A most satisfying state of mind,
A peaceful empty head.
I lay my aching head
Upon a pillow made of feathers
My all-engulfing problems
Drifting gently in a haze
In foetal calm I float –
My mind takes time to go and play –
Out among the clouds
The sun is shining bright today.
When I was a little child the safest place to be
Was snuggling in my mother's arms,
Sitting on her knee.
Now, though, I'm an adult
And I have no guarantee
That there's comfort, still,
And solace available to me.

I lay my grown-up head
Upon a pillow made of feathers
And I'm back there for a moment
And we're smiling happily.
My pillow gives me respite,
Doesn't question, doesn't see,
Allows me to renew my strength
And wake relaxed and free.

My Ancestors

The years roll on relentlessly
And clouds obscure my memory
Beloved faces come to me:
My dear departed family.
Their struggles are now history
Compiled upon my family tree.
Their hopes and fears for all to see,
Laced richly with humanity.
Their tears and wars and harmony,
Their humour and simplicity,
Intelligence and decency,
Wisdom, faith and courtesy.
A large assembly watches me
And whispers from eternity.
Somehow I feel they're close to me
Anticipating eagerly.
I cannot stem my welling pride
For those who cried and tried and died.
Who persevered unsatisfied
And now in bliss reside.

Earn the Gift

To walk amid a place of peace,
To look into a face of love,
To seek and win a sweet release
and soar in blueness far above
I have to live and stretch my heart
In yearning trial and icy scold.
In clammy sweat and bitter part
I'll earn the gift that can't be sold.

Jesus is Real

Jesus is somewhere walking, talking.
Jesus is real like you and me.
He is knocking, waving, calling
Saying to you "come follow me".
Jesus is teaching, working, building.
He is the way to heaven above.
He hopes you'll listen, pray and follow
Because He is kind and full of love.
Jesus is near you whispering, answering
So don't be afraid to kneel and pray.
He will comfort you, heal you, save you.
Welcome Him in this very day.

Hey, You With The Frown

Relax those muscles,
Let them rest.
You need to look happy
To look your best.
If you change your expression
You'll soften your mood
And this will improve
Your attitude.
Don't get me wrong.
I think you are great.
I know that you're stressed,
You've a lot on your plate.
We all have our off days.
I thought you seemed down.
Well somebody cares
So get rid of the frown.

A Few Grey Hairs

A few grey hairs
In a clump on my head
Keep me looking in the mirror
With a feeling of dread.
I close my eyes
And another one appears
Signalling the march
Of the advancing years.
Each non-conformist strand
Was caused by stress
From dealing with emotions
In a muddle and a mess.
Each white hair represents
Some wisdom gained
So imagine how I'll look
When I am fully trained.

No Money Again

Every month it happens,
A day of dark despair.
I go to draw some money
And I'm told there's nothing there.
I'm getting quite inventive
In my quest to earn more cash.
Still, I never have a surplus
That can grow into a stash.
There is more to life than money –
It can't buy happiness –
But it sure could make life pleasant,
Free from worries, debts and stress.
I'll pay all that's outstanding,
Although I can't say when.
I am down but not defeated
And I'll rise to spend again!

Printed in Great Britain
by Amazon.co.uk, Ltd.,
Marston Gate.